AF367489

Practical guide to the rules
Incoterms 2020

Rights and obligations on the goods in international trade

David Soler

Index

The Incoterms 2020 rules

Practical guide to the rules
Incoterms 2020

1 International trade

For centuries, the international goods trade has been one of the main driving forces in the world economy. From the great empires of ancient times to the international capitalist corporations, all economic systems have used trade as a system to articulate the extraction of raw materials from some territories and, in turn, to introduce in these same territories the consumption of products manufactured in other regions.

With the globalization process experienced by the world economy since the 1970s, the increase in international transactions has reached unprecedented levels. Thus, while world GDP increased fourfold during the period 1970-2013, international trade increased tenfold. This intensification meant that while exports represented around 13% of world GDP in 1970, in just over three decades, in 2013, they accounted for almost 30%.

However, the trend towards a globalized economy shows a lower growth in international trade in the period 2014-2020. Beyond the typical downturns in demand, market saturation and financial recessions, it was inevitable that this growth which seemed to be expanding infinitely became limited by crises related to the depletion of fossil fuels, the environmental emergency that looms over the planet and, very significantly, by critical situations related to it, such as the one derived from the pandemic generated by Covid-19. We can say that the economic, environmental and social crises at the beginning of the 2020s are manifestations of a global crisis that is essentially generated by certain production and consumption models which international trade has played a fundamental role in developing.

On the other hand, the sustained growth that international trade has kept up for centuries has been possible because, in addition to major investments by private companies, particularly in modes of transport, at the same time, the public administrations in the majority of countries have made huge financial investments in logistics infrastructure with a high degree of technological development and automation in their systems. In turn, these infrastructures have required a significant use of natural resources and, often, of large tracts of land.

Finally, the combinatorial analysis of the increase and diversification of the flow of goods between countries and economic regions, the availability of technological resources, improvements in transport safety and quality and the reduction in transit times have meant that international trade processes and procedures have evolved progressively up to the volumes that we know today.

2   Rules for international trade

Over time, the complexity of international trade transactions has necessitated the development of a combination of business and professional figures with high degrees of specialization. Some are focused on the freight transport processes, others focus on administrative and customs processing, others on the financial aspects of the operations and still others on covering the economic risks involved in each operation, amongst the most relevant.

Pooling the interests of the buyer and seller in an international sales transaction and combining these interests with the professional sectors that must make the operation viable has required the articulation of clear and precise procedures between numerous organizations, countries and cultures. From this need derives the active participation of the international corporate organizations in which the companies that participate in each sector are grouped, among others:

- International Maritime Organization (IMO).
- International Air Transport Association (IATA).
- International Road Transport Union (IRU).
- Intergovernmental Organization for International Carriage by Rail (OTIF).
- International Federation of Freight Forwarders Associations (FIATA).
- International Association of Professional Customs Agents (ASAPRA).

Numerous international standards or recommendations have been derived from the articulation of procedures that have required the involvement of other supranational organisations such as the World Trade Organization (WTO), the International Monetary Fund (IMF) or the International Chamber of Commerce (ICC), for example.

<table>
<tr><td>● ●   What are Incoterms rules</td></tr>
</table>

They are intended to demarcate the rights and obligations of the parties involved in the international sale of a product with regard to these five aspects:

- Obligations of the buyer and the seller.
- Costs borne by each party.
- Responsibility on the goods.
- Customs clearance.
- Place and time of delivery of the goods.

These regulations and recommendations arise from the fact that international sale of goods transactions, unlike those carried out within the same country, involve a series of procedures and technical and administrative conditions that decisively affect the way in which the commercial transaction has to be agreed and developed and, particularly, the physical delivery of the goods.

In general, these procedures and conditions fall under two management areas: financial and logistics.

Having extensive knowledge of financial management of international trade and a solid professional experience are the best guarantee for choosing, for example, the means of payment that offers greater security in each transaction.

Likewise, knowledge of international trade logistics and being able to count on the collaboration of professional experts are the best supports to plan a logistics process in which the goods will move through storage areas, ports or goods terminals and use different transport modes or vehicles. A scenario in which it is also necessary to know the workings of the documentary processes that affect the goods in the country of origin and destination and where the slightest aspect can have considerable significance.

So, for example, the distance and incidents that may arise in the journey between the country in which the selling company is located and that of the buyer may increase transport costs and risks. An international sales transaction may become unfeasible, among other reasons, because of the freight price, the difficul-

freight

Remuneration that the company responsible for operating the mode of transport (sea, road or air) receives for the transport and delivery of the goods or for the hire of a vessel or part thereof. It may be paid or due, by which it is established whether the payment is made at origin or destination, respectively. The most commonly used calculation basis is the ton but the cubic meter is used if the calculation is by volume.

ties involved in customs procedures or the continuous handling of goods (in transhipment between modes of transport, in transfers at port terminals, etc.).

international sales contract

It is the commercial document that two or more parties sign as a formal expression of an agreement for the international sale of goods. In addition to describing the buying and selling parties and trading companies or agencies that may be involved, as well as the goods subject of the transaction, the terms of the agreement are set forth in detail, in particular all possible deadlines or times, the amount, terms of payment, the place and delivery terms of the goods (type of transport, packaging, etc), the responsibilities that each party assumes and any other consideration relating to the operation that they wish to express. The Incoterms rule that was agreed must also be indicated in the contract for the international sale of goods.

Another aspect worthy of consideration concerns the legislation that must cover an international trade transaction. Each country or economic-fiscal area may have legislation that provides legal coverage within the territory in which it has been approved but that cannot be applied outside its domain, which is why the difficulty arises in deciding which regulation should be applicable to the transaction.

Likewise, factors relating to the culture of each place should always be taken into account. This includes language, customs and business practices, as well as social environments. All these aspects can be very different between the parties and so give rise to different interpretations and assessments of their obligations and the existence or not of breaches in the conditions of delivery of the goods (place and time of delivery, packaging used, etc.) and on whom the responsibility should fall for same.

In the first decades of the twentieth century, given the evidence that it was necessary to establish a regulation that would serve as a reference to regulate this type of situations, the International Chamber of Commerce (ICC) developed the Incoterms® rules (acronym for *International Commercial Terms)* in 1936. The main purpose of this initiative was to contribute to legal certainty in international sale of goods transactions and to the standardization of the conditions of delivery of same. Since their first publication, these rules have been periodically reviewed and adapted to successive changes in the sphere of international trade, while the most recent version at the time of editing this guide recognizes in the same way the application of the Incoterms rules to transactions conducted in the same country or economic-fiscal area, provided that the parties so agree.[1]

This implies the need to understand and use these rules correctly, for while their application is not mandatory, their contribution to the understanding between the selling and buying parties makes them recommendable. In such a case, the companies must reflect this clearly in the sales contract by referring to the version they are invoking, i.e. the most recent.

....

[1] For more information on the description and use of Incoterms rules, see *Incoterms 2020 rules user manual,* by Alfonso Cabrera Cánovas (Marge Books, Barcelona, 2020).

3   Purpose and scope of the Incoterms rules

They are intended to demarcate the rights and obligations of the parties to an international sales contract with regard to the delivery terms of the goods subject of the transaction. This is basically determined by answering five key questions:

- Which obligations each party (buyer and seller) undertakes in accordance with what is agreed

logistics chain

It is the process of planning, management and control of the flows of materials and products, information and services related to this process. It identifies the procurement, production and distribution sub-processes and includes internal and external movements as well as import and export operations.

upon in the sales contract in relation to the delivery of the goods.

- Which costs each party bears in relation to the hiring of transport and the set of operations that may take place in the logistics chain (packing, loading and stowing in vehicles, unstowing and unloading, etc.).

- Which party bears the risk of the goods during their transportation, their insurance cost, and to or from which point in the journey there is coverage by this insurance, in the event that it has been taken out.

customs clearance

Set of logistics procedures and operations that must be carried out on the goods in a customs area to manage the physical entry or exit of same in a certain territory (country, economic-fiscal area, etc.).

- Which party is obliged to carry out customs clearance, if it is necessary.
- Which are the place and time of delivery of the goods and the transfer of risks from the selling company to the buyer.

It should be noted, however, that Incoterms rules do not constitute a sales contract in themselves, since they do not regulate certain aspects that are decisive for a commercial transaction; for example, the legislation that should apply in case of breach of the commercial conditions that are agreed.

3.1　Aspects regulated by the Incoterms rules

The Incoterms rules define under ten headings the commitments that the selling and buying companies may be subject to regarding the delivery of the goods:

- **Obligations of the selling company**

  1. Delivery of the goods and the commercial invoice under the conditions agreed in the sales contract.

2. Licenses, authorizations, security accreditations and other formalities, including export or import clearance.
3. Contracts of carriage and insurance.
4. Delivery of the goods.
5. Transfer of risks.
6. Cost sharing.
7. Notification to the buying company of the delivery of the goods.
8. Documents and proof of delivery.
9. Checking, packing and marking of goods.
10. Help with information and related costs.

- **Obligations of the buying company**

1. Payment of the price of the goods agreed upon in the sales contract.
2. Licenses, authorizations, security accreditations and other formalities, including export or import clearance.
3. Contracts of carriage and insurance.
4. Reception of the goods.
5. Transfer of risks.
6. Cost sharing.

7. Notification to the selling company of the reception of the goods.

8. Documents and proof of delivery.

9. Inspection of goods.

10. Assist the selling party with the information requested and related costs.

contract of carriage

By means of the contract of carriage, a natural or legal person known as a carrier undertakes to carry something while another, called a shipper, undertakes to pay a price for this transport service. As there are obligations for both parties, this type of contract is known as bilateral or synallagmatic.

The contract of carriage establishes the price stipulated for the service and that the merchandise object of same must reach its destination without damage or reduction in its nature, with the possibility of establishing other clauses such as the agreed delivery time at destination.

3.2   *Aspects not regulated by the Incoterms rules*

The following aspects, essential for the commercial transaction of the sale of goods, are outside the scope of the Incoterms rules although their negotiation may be affected by the agreed delivery conditions:

- Contract of carriage conditions between the selling or buying company and the carrier.

freight insurance contract

Contract by which one company (the insurer) undertakes, in exchange for a premium, to compensate another (the insured) in the event that one of the risks provided for in this contract occurs, causing damage, losses or delays in the goods transported and for a sum also determined in same. For the company that owns the goods, this is damage insurance, while for the carrier it is civil liability insurance.

PRACTICAL GUIDE TO THE INCOTERMS 2020 RULES

The selling and buying parties of an international sales transaction must understand and use these rules correctly. Although their application is not mandatory, they are essential for an understanding between all the agents and professional teams involved in international trade.

International supply chain agents

- Exporting and importing companies.
- Freight forwarders – Air freight forwarders.
- Shipping agents.
- Customs agents.
- International logistics operators.
- Road hauliers.
- Railway operators.
- Shipping companies.
- Air cargo operators.
- Insurers.
- Financial services.
- Foreign trade consultants.
- Warehousers.
- Distributors.
- Security services.
- Security advisory companies.
- Transport centre management teams.
- Commercial port management teams.
- Heads of foreign trade in the public administration.

- Transfer of ownership of the goods.
- Sales price, payment means and terms.
- Applicable regulations in case of breach of contract, its resolution and jurisdiction.
- Exemption from liability on the goods.

Therefore, both parties must agree on the conditions relating to these areas and express them properly and as precisely as possible in the sales contract.

supply chain

It brings together the set of activities of an organization aimed at satisfying the demand for products and services, from the initial raw materials and information requirements up to the delivery to the final user and recovery of waste materials that may have been generated in the process.

Although the Incoterms rules do not expressly regulate international means of payment, there is a close relationship between both which must be taken into account in order to avoid malfunctions that make payment of the transaction difficult and to be able to properly handle certain means of payment such as documentary, for example. In the event that a documentary credit is used as a means of payment, the obligations regarding delivery conditions assumed by the selling company in the sales contract must necessarily coincide with those undertaken documentarily in the formalization of this credit.

Note that the Incoterms rules are only applicable to contracts for the sale of goods, so the marketing of services is beyond their scope.

4   The Incoterms 2020 rules

The Incoterms 2020 rules comprise eleven rules that are identified by their initials in English. Table 1 shows the list of these acronyms with their corresponding descriptions in English and Spanish.

From the perspective of the obligations and responsibilities assumed by the selling company, the Incoterms rules can be classified into four categories that group these rules according to the initial letter

THE INCOTERMS 2020 RULES	
Acronym	Description
EXW	Ex works
FCA	Free carrier
FAS	Free alongside ship
FOB	Free on board
CFR	Cost and freight
CIF	Cost, insurance and freight
CPT	Carriage paid to
CIP	Carriage and insurance paid to
DAP	Delivered at place
DPU	Delivered at place unloaded
DDP	Delivered duty paid

Table 1. Acronyms and descriptions corresponding to the Incoterms 2020 rules.

of their corresponding acronyms and according to the place of delivery of the goods:

- **E Rules:** delivery at origin in the premises of the selling company

    The selling company makes the goods available to the buyer in its own premises.

- **F Rules:** delivery at origin without payment of the main transport by the selling company

    The selling company delivers the goods in the mode of transport hired by the buyer or in the place that the latter designates at origin.

- **C Rules:** delivery at origin with payment of the main transport by the selling company

    The selling company contracts the main transport up to destination but delivers the goods and transfers the risks at origin.

- **D Rules:** delivery at destination

    The selling company bears all the costs and risks necessary to transport the goods to their destination.

5 Risks and costs

From the moment the selling company initiates the actions necessary to make the goods available to the buyer, a series of risks and costs resulting from multiple factors arises, such as the distance between the points of origin and destination, the nature and type of goods (loose packages, palletized cargo, bulk, containerised load, etc), the mode or modes of transport used, etc. Among the main risks and costs are the following:

- At the point of origin of the goods

    - Verification of the goods, packaging and configuration of the loading units.
    - Loading, stowing and securing in the mode of inland transport.
    - Inland transport (in the country of origin).
    - Customs clearance at departure.
    - Handling of goods in the port or terminal of departure.
    - Main transport.
    - Insurance.

- At the point of destination of the goods

  - Handling of goods in the port or terminal of entry.
  - Customs clearance at entry.
  - Inland transport (in the country of destination).
  - Reception, unloading and unstowing of goods.
  - Insurance.

Generally, the selling company bears all risks up to the named place of delivery and on the agreed

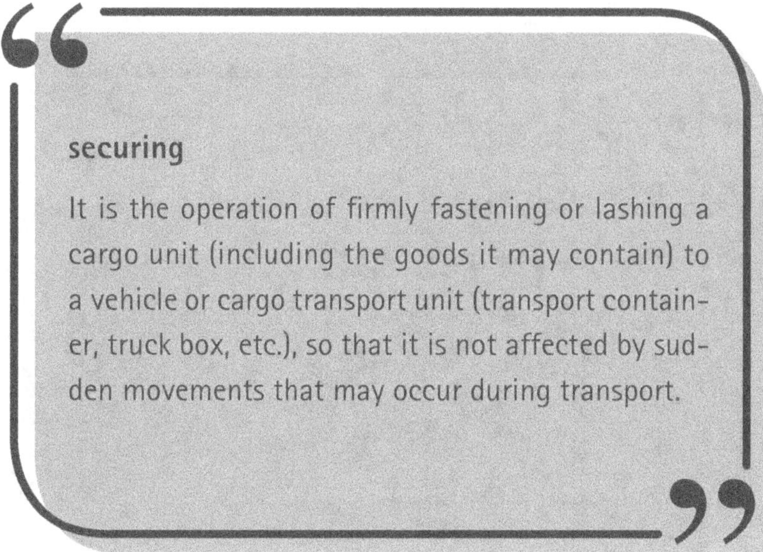

securing

It is the operation of firmly fastening or lashing a cargo unit (including the goods it may contain) to a vehicle or cargo transport unit (transport container, truck box, etc.), so that it is not affected by sudden movements that may occur during transport.

date or time. The possibilities with respect to the point of delivery are very diverse, from delivery at origin or destination up to delivery at a certain point of the route that the goods will take (in the departure or arrival terminals, on board the ship, on a distribution platform, etc.) and on a certain date or time.

It is at the point of delivery when the transfer of risks occurs, so from then on any possible risks and damages to the goods during transport, and all those arising from the logistics chain from that moment on, are borne by the buying company.

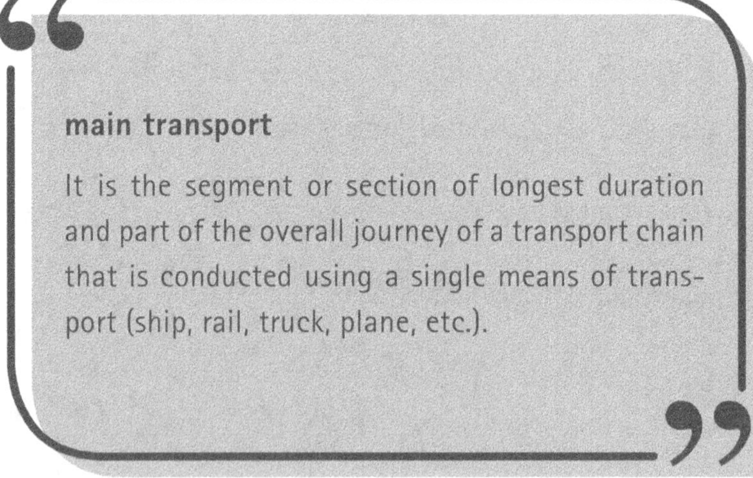

main transport

It is the segment or section of longest duration and part of the overall journey of a transport chain that is conducted using a single means of transport (ship, rail, truck, plane, etc.).

Similarly, as far as costs are concerned, the selling company must bear all those arising from the delivery of the goods at the place and time agreed upon.

Thus, when agreeing the conditions of the sales contract, the selling and buying companies must analyze, assess and agree with the maximum precision:

- What are the risks and costs arising from the sale of goods transaction.
- Which party should bear such risks and costs and to what extent.

stowage

It is the operation of moving goods, by means of proper handling, distribution and placement in a means of transport so as to avoid or minimize possible damage to them, facilitate unloading and protect people or things.

- In which precise place and point the transfer of risks from the selling company to the buyer takes place.

6   Contracts of carriage

The Incoterms rules, despite the inescapable implications of their application in terms of hiring transport, concern only aspects related to the sale of the goods.

Contracts of carriage are included in the corresponding regulatory requirements according to the

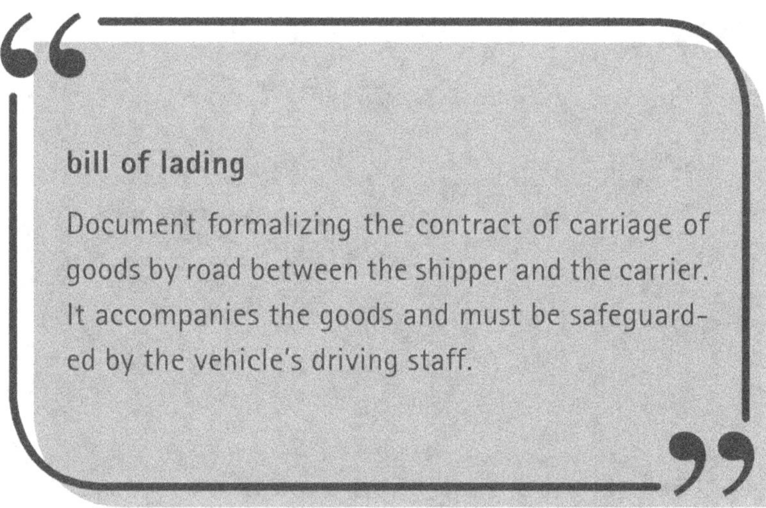

mode or modes of transport used in each case and their scope of application.

Apart from the agreed Incoterms rules, in the contract of carriage only the conditions that have been agreed between the carrier and the shipper, its customer, whether buyer or seller in the commercial transaction, are applicable.

means of transport

It is the type of vehicle used for transportation. Each mode of transport has a specific typology:

- Air transport: airplane, helicopter, etc.
- Road transport: truck, van, etc.
- Rail transport: train.
- Maritime and river transport: ship, boat, barge, etc.
- Pipeline transport: pipes.

It is a common practice that transport quotes are requested indicating the agreed Incoterms rule as well as specifying this rule in the consignment notes as an indication of who is responsible for bearing the transportation cost.

7   Insurance policies

Regarding the contracting of transport insurance, it is only mandatory under CIF and CIP conditions. In both cases, the selling company must take out an insurance that covers the risks of the buyer in relation to the transportation of the goods and with the coverage and conditions that these rules specify (both parties may, by mutual agreement, extend the coverage or specify the conditions of the insurance).

Although in the rest of the terms of delivery, each party decides if it wishes to insure the transaction and under what conditions, there is no doubt that all transportation is subject to certain risks that recommend taking out an insurance policy to cover what each party has taken on, according to the place of delivery and transfer of risk that was agreed.

8   Export and import customs clearance

These procedures, when applicable (this is not the case in sales transactions carried out in the same country or economic-fiscal area), involve managing the corresponding customs clearances and their documentation.

In all cases, the selling company (exporter) always takes responsability for export customs clearance, except under EXW conditions.

Likewise, the import customs clearance always falls on the buying company (importer), except under DDP conditions.

9   Modes of transport

Depending on the mode of transport for which they are designed, the Incoterms rules are classified, in the 2020 version, into the following groups:

- **Multi-purpose or multi-modal Incoterms rules**
  They are suitable for any operation involving road, rail, air or multimodal transport, including containerized multimodal transport with maritime transport phase, as well as the combina-

multimodality and multimodal transport

Multimodality facilitates the organisation of transport using different modes on the same route or in a given geographical area.

Thus, multimodal transport is a combined transport system in which there is no breakdown of the load unit and in the main or long-haul transport phase a succession of different means is used: truck-train, truck-ship, truck-ship-train or any other possible combination. All this under a single contract of carriage between the transport operator and the shipper.

tion of any of these modes (except port-to-port maritime). This category includes the rules:

EXW	Ex works
FCA	Free carrier
CPT	Carriage paid to
CIP	Carriage and insurance paid to
DAP	Delivered at place
DPU	Delivered at place unloaded
DDP	Delivered duty paid

- **Incoterms rules for maritime and inland waterways transport**

  They are suitable for all those operations that involve transporting non-containerized, break-bulk, bulk, etc., general cargo from port to port. This category includes the rules:

FAS	Free alongside ship
FOB	Free on board
CFR	Cost and freight
CIF	Cost, insurance and freight

The Incoterms 2020 rules

	EXW	FCA seller's premises	FCA named place
Packaging	●	●	●
Other export costs: documents, certifications...	●	●	●
Loading the goods into the initial transport vehicle	○	●	●
Export clearance	○	●	●
Initial transport	○	○	●
Transport to terminal	○	○	●
Costs in terminal of origin: THC, taxes and others	○	○	○
Free on board	○	○	○
Main transport	○	○	○
Transport insurance	◦	◦	◦
Unloading in terminal	○	○	○
Destination terminal costs: THC, taxes and others	○	○	○
Import clearance	○	○	○
Transportation from terminal to destination	○	○	○
Unloading of goods from the final transport vehicle	○	○	○

● At the expense of the selling company.

○ At the expense of the buying company.

FAS	FOB	CFR	CIF	CPT	CIP	DAP	DPU	DDP

● ◎ It is not obligatory to take out insurance as a condition of an Incoterms rule but the party, either seller or buyer, who mainly bears the transport risks and should consider taking out insurance is indicated. In general, it is at the buyer's convenience from EXW to CPT, while it will mainly suit the seller from DAP to DDP.

The Incoterms 2020 rules

EXW
FCA
FAS
FOB
CFR
CIF
CPT
CIP
DAP
DPU
DDP

Delivery at origin in the premises of the selling company

These delivery conditions are the ones which mean fewest obligations for the selling company and are expressed only by the multimodal EXW rule which may be applied using any mode of transport or possible combinations among them (road, sea, air and rail).

EXW (ex works)

Place of delivery and transfer of risks

Under EXW conditions, the selling company fulfils its commitment to deliver the goods and transfers the risks on them by making them available to the buying company in its own premises or in another named place (factory, warehouse, depot, distribution platform, etc.), without loading them on the transport vehicle that will have been sent by the buying party.

To avoid incidents in the delivery, it is advisable that the buying company include the loading operation (including stowage and mooring, as appropriate) when hiring the transportation service and ensures that the carrier has the necessary means for this operation or, failing that, puts them at its disposal.

The selling company bears the costs of packaging the goods for the shipment, which must be properly packed and labelled.

The buying company must provide the seller with proof of receipt of the goods.

Customs clearance

Where applicable, it is the responsibility of the buying company to carry out the customs export procedures in the country of origin as well as the import procedures in the country of destination and, where appropriate, transit procedures through third countries.

The selling company must provide the buyer with the documentation it requests for carrying out such procedures and the payment of their costs.

Modes of transport and goods

The EXW rule is multimodal and may be applied to any mode of transport that is used or possible combinations among them (road, sea, air and rail).

The buying company takes charge of the entire transportation and set of operations that make up the logistics chain up to destination, their risks and costs.

EXW is an Incoterms rule that is used particularly in parcel shipments and small easy-to-handle loads, in sales transactions on a national level or within the same economic-fiscal region, such as the European Union.

Insurance

Since the EXW rule implies a minimum of obligations for the selling company, it is up to the buyer to decide whether to insure the risks of the transaction.

EXW (ex works)

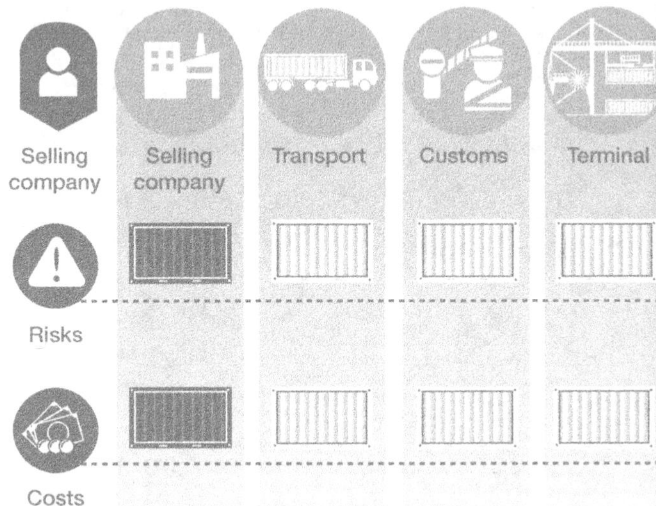

The operation of loading the transport vehicle is always the responsibility of the buying company, so it must be done by it or the carrier contracted by it, even when the goods are to be combined with other shipments to form larger cargo units or full truck loads.

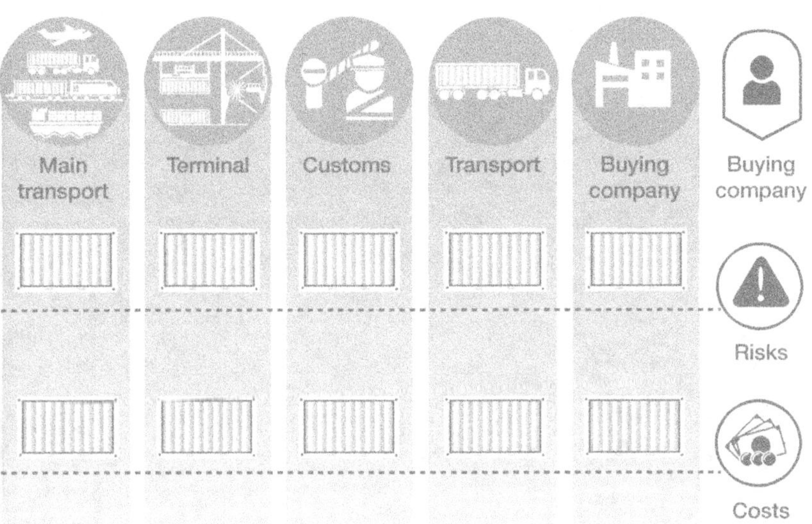

The selling company delivers the goods by making them available
to the buyer in its own premises without loading them on the vehicle
sent by the buying company. The latter bears all costs and risks from
that moment on.

F

**FCA
FAS
FOB**

Delivery at origin without payment of the main transport

These delivery conditions establish that the selling company must deliver the goods for transportation in the country of origin, in accordance with the instructions of the buyer.

This group comprises the FCA multimodal and the FAS and FOB maritime rules.

FCA (free carrier)

Place of delivery and transfer of risks

Under FCA conditions, the selling company fulfils its obligations and transfers the risks by delivering the goods to the carrier contracted by the buyer at the designated place in the country of origin. The delivery of the goods can be arranged in two ways:

- **FCA seller's premises,** when it assumes the loading of the goods in its own premises on board the transport vehicle hired by the buyer. From that moment on, the buyer bears the costs and risks on the goods.

- **FCA named place,** when the selling company assumes a first shipment up to an agreed point (an air cargo center; a port or railway container terminal, freight forwarder warehouse, etc.) and delivers the goods on the vehicle ready for unloading. From that moment on, the buyer bears the costs and risks and is responsible for unloading the goods from the vehicle at the designated delivery place.

In both cases, the selling company must provide the buyer with the standard proof of delivery of the goods, which the latter is obliged to accept.

Customs clearance

The application of the FCA rule requires the selling party to carry out export clearance, where applicable, in the country of origin's customs.

For its part, the buying company shall be responsible for the import customs procedures in the country of destination and, where appropriate, transit procedures through third countries.

The selling company must provide the buyer with the documentation it requests for carrying out such procedures and the payment of their costs.

Modes of transport and goods

The FCA rule is multimodal and may be applied to any mode of transport that is used or possible combinations among them (road, sea, air and rail).

It is advisable to use the FCA rule if the goods travel by container, either a full container (in which case the FOB rule is not advised) or a part load. It is also true if full truck load or groupage road transport is used.

Insurance

The FCA rule does not oblige taking out an insurance policy but both companies must decide whether to insure the risks of the operation, the seller until the delivery of the goods and the buyer from that moment on, when it assumes the set of remaining operations in the logistics chain up to the destination.

FCA seller's premises (free carrier)

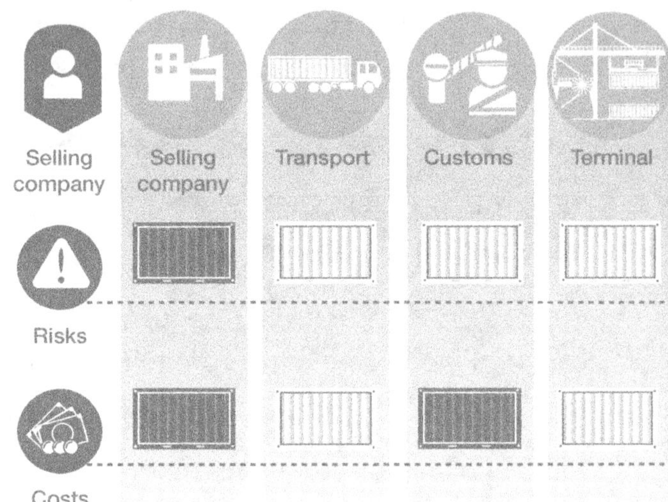

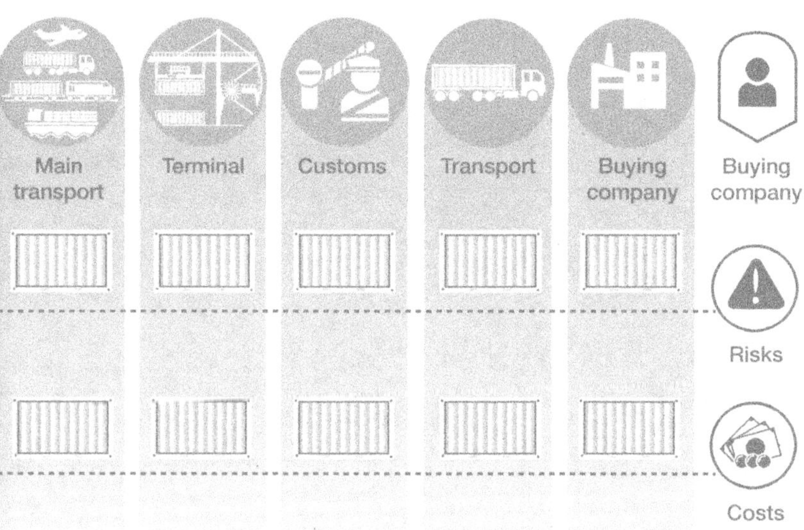

The selling company delivers the goods, cleared for export, once loaded on the vehicle that the buying company sends to its facilities. From that moment on, the following costs and risks are all borne by the buying company.

FCA named place (free carrier)

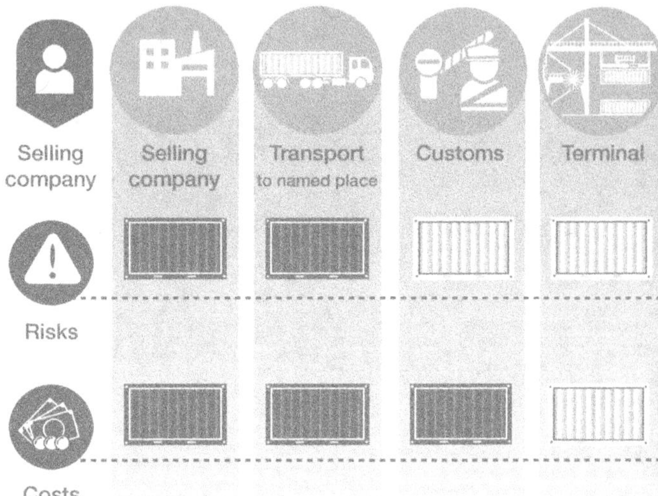

The selling company bears the costs and risks until the goods
are put in the designated place (warehouse, terminal, etc.), without
being unloaded from the arrival vehicle and cleared for export.
From that moment on, the following costs and risks are all borne
by the buying company.

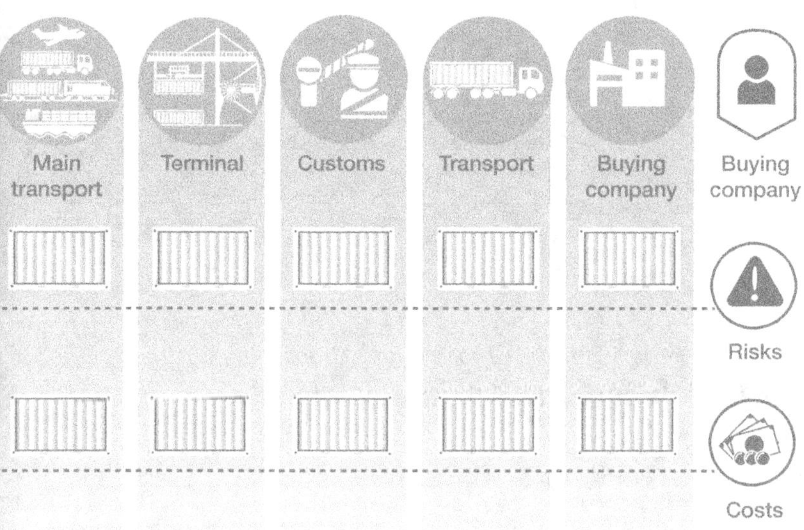

The selling company delivers the goods to the agreed place (without unloading them from the vehicle with which they are transported) and cleared for export. From that moment on, the following costs and risks are all borne by the buying company.

FCA (FREE CARRIER)

FAS (free alongside ship)

Place of delivery and transfer of risks

Under FAS conditions, the selling company complies with its obligations and transmits the risks by delivering the goods alongside the vessel booked by the buyer in the terminal of the designated port of embarkation and on the agreed date. From that moment on, the costs and risks of the entire logistics chain, including loading, stowage or trim on the ship, fall on the buying company.

The selling company must provide the buyer with the standard proof of delivery of the goods, in this case issued by a maritime or port operator.

Whenever the buying company requests it, the seller must provide the necessary assistance so that the former, at its own cost and risk, can obtain the bill of lading or any other maritime document.

Customs clearance

The application of the FAS rule requires the selling party to carry out export clearance, where applicable, in the country of origin's customs.

For its part, the buying company shall be responsible for the import customs procedures in the country of destination and, where appropriate, transit procedures through third countries.

The selling company must provide the buyer with the documentation it requests for carrying out such procedures and the payment of their costs.

Modes of transport and goods

The Incoterms FAS rule is preferably used when it comes to the sale of bulk goods, capital goods, heavy machinery, large volumes, etc. and maritime or inland waterway transport will be used for their shipment.

(Continued on page 66)

FAS (FREE ALONGSIDE SHIP)

FAS (free alongside ship)

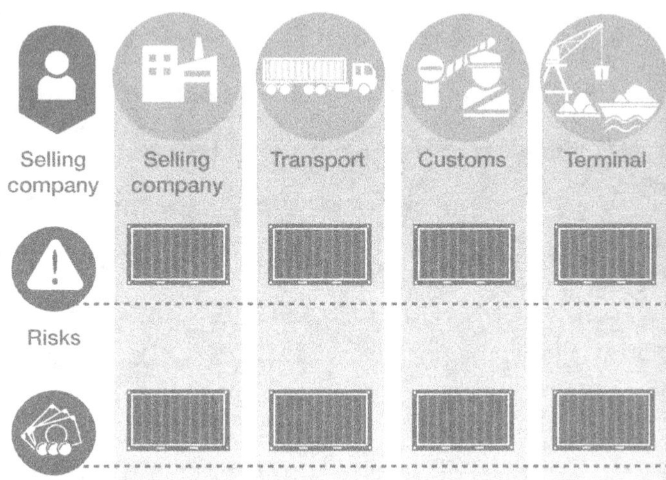

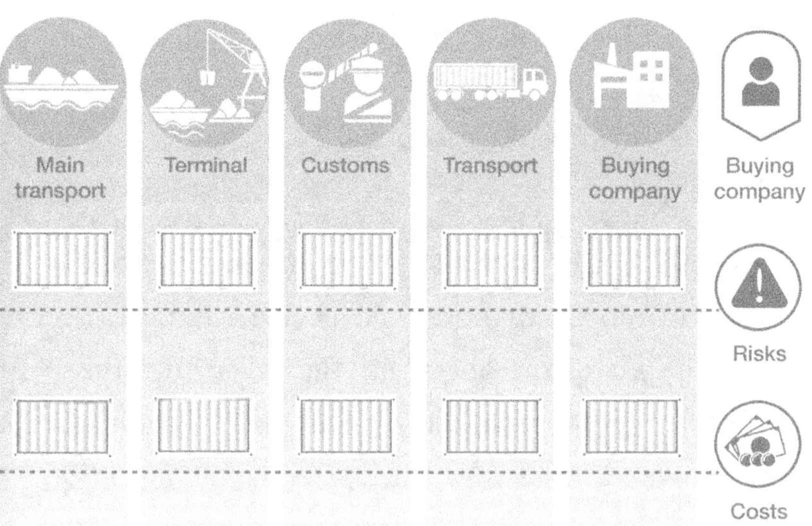

The selling company bears the costs and risks until the goods
are cleared for export and placed alongside the vessel in the
terminal of the port of embarkation. From that moment on,
the costs and risks (loading on board the ship, stowage, transport
and others at destination) all fall on the buying company.

FAS (FREE ALONGSIDE SHIP)

(Continued from page 63)

The FAS rule is not advisable if the goods travel in a container, instead the use of the FCA rule is advisable.

Insurance

The FAS rule does not oblige taking out an insurance policy but both companies must decide whether to insure the risks of the operation, the seller until the delivery of the goods and the buyer from that moment on, when it assumes the set of remaining operations in the logistics chain up to the destination.

FOB (free on board)

Place of delivery and transfer of risks

This rule, frequently used in international sales operations, establishes that the selling company fulfils its obligations and transfers the risks by delivering the goods on board the vessel booked by the buyer in the named port of embarkation.

Even if the buying company has booked the freight under *liner terms* and, therefore, this includes the costs of loading and stowage, the transfer of risks from the selling company only takes place when the goods have been placed on board the ship.

The seller must provide the buyer with proof of delivery of the goods on board the ship in the port of origin, which in this case may consist of a bill of lading issued by the ship's first officer.

The standard proof of delivery is the bill of lading which formalizes the maritime contract of carriage and which can also be managed by the selling company freight collect.

In any case, provided that the buying company requests it, the seller must provide the necessary assistance so that the former, at its own cost and risk, can obtain the bill of lading or any other maritime document.

It is appropriate to use the FOB rule when sales transactions occur during the sea journey since it provides that delivery must be made on board the ship or "by providing the goods so delivered", i.e. once shipped and given that the bill of lading acts as a negotiable instrument.

Customs clearance

The application of the FOB rule requires the selling party to carry out export clearance, where applicable, in the country of origin's customs.

For its part, the buying company shall be responsible for the import customs procedures in the country of destination and, where appropriate, transit procedures through third countries.

The selling company must provide the buyer with the documentation it requests for carrying out such procedures and the payment of their costs.

Modes of transport and goods

The use of the FOB rule extends to the sale of all types of goods, from those which are transported as bulk, breakbulk or general cargo (boxes, drums, bales, sacks, etc., in single units or grouped on pallets), heavy equipment, bulky parts or containers, among others, provided that maritime transport is to be used for their shipment.

The FOB rule is not advisable if the goods travel in a container, in which case the use of the FCA rule is more advisable.

Insurance

The FOB rule does not oblige taking out an insurance policy but both companies have to decide whether

(Continued on page 74)

FOB (free on board)

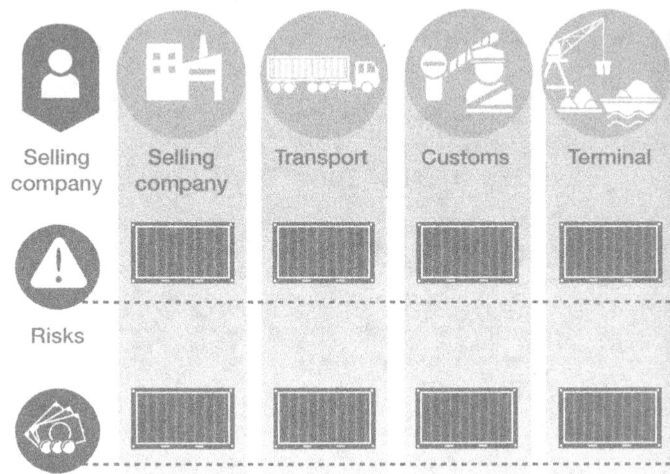

PRACTICAL GUIDE TO THE INCOTERMS 2020 RULES

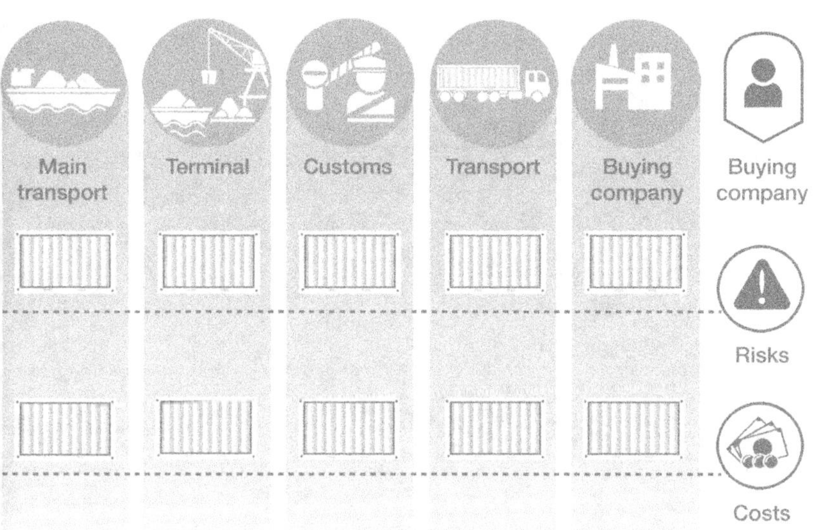

The selling company bears the costs and risks until the goods
are cleared for export and placed on board the ship in the port
of embarkation. From that moment on, the costs and risks (transport
and others at destination) all fall on the buying company.

FOB (free on board): with container

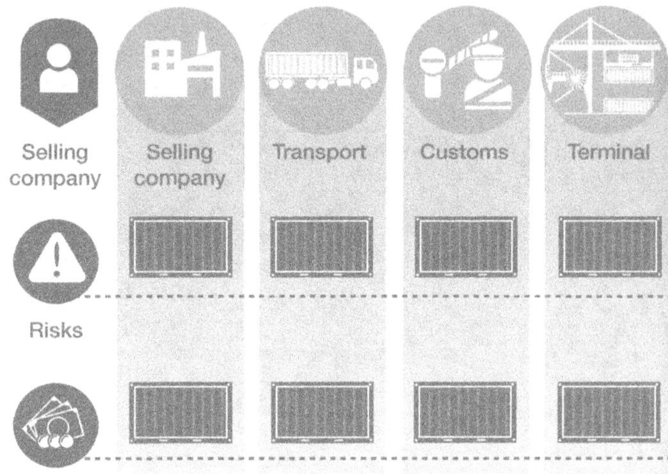

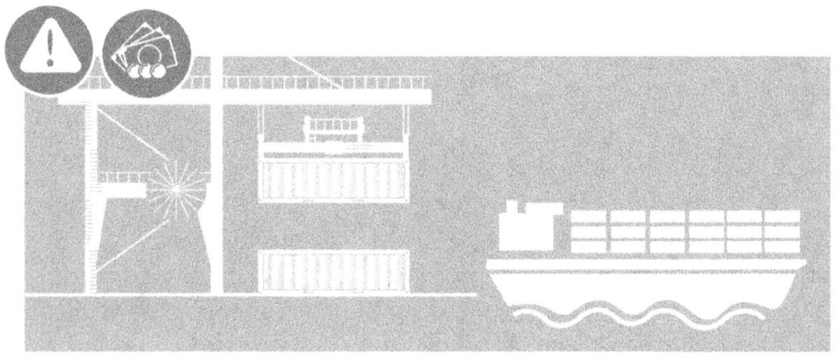

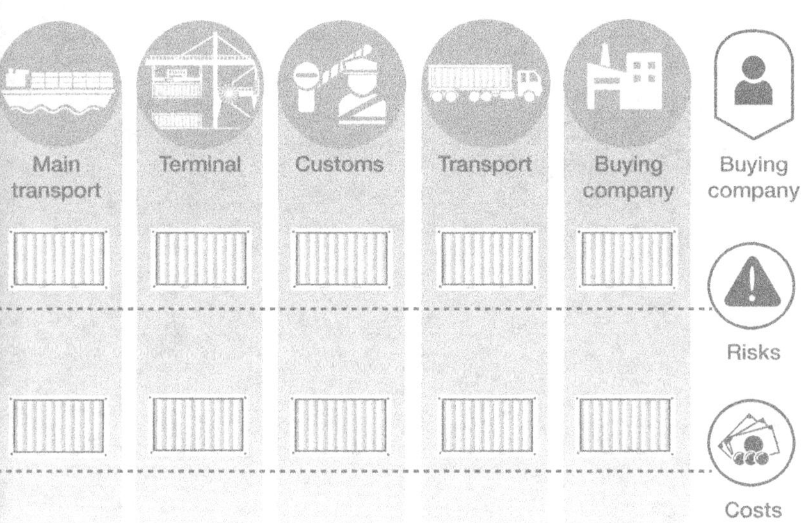

The selling company bears the costs and risks until the container is dispatched for export and placed on board the ship in the port of embarkation. From this point on, the costs and risks (transport and others at destination) all fall on the buying company.

FOB (FREE ON BOARD)

(Continued from page 69)

to insure the risks of the operation, the seller until the delivery of the goods on board the ship and the buyer from that moment on, when it assumes the set of remaining operations in the logistics chain up to the destination.

C

CFR   CPT
CIF   CIP

Delivery at origin with payment of the main transport

These delivery conditions are mainly characterized by the fact that, although the seller bears the cost of the main transport of the goods, the risks arising therefrom fall on the buyer, since the delivery and transfer of risks take place at origin, as is the case with the rules in groups E and F. The difference is that, under C conditions, it is the selling company that books the transport, thus assuming more costs, though not more risks.

This group comprises the CFR and CIF maritime Incoterms rules and the CPT and CIP multimodal ones.

CFR (cost and freight)

Place of delivery and transfer of risks

Under CFR, the selling company is obliged to bear all costs and freight necessary to transport the goods to the named port of destination, without unloading the goods from the ship. However, delivery and transfer of risk takes place once the goods have been placed on board the vessel. In the event of one or more transhipments of the goods in different ports during transportation, the goods are considered to be delivered in the first of them, the port of embarkation.

Since the selling company bears a significant part of the transport costs, with regard to the contractual clauses of loading and unloading or maritime transport shipping terms, it can book the freight under LIFO conditions *(liner in, free out),* which will include the cost of loading and stowage operations of the goods in the port of origin, while the unstowing and unloading at the port of destination will be borne by the buying company or its consignee.

Using the CFR rule, it is also possible to agree that the costs of unloading at the port of destination are borne by the selling company, for which it is necessary to indicate the CFR *landed* condition and agree on the operation with the shipping company.

The selling company must provide the buyer with the standard transport document (originals of the maritime *bill of lading* or BL) which allows the latter to pick up the goods at the named port of destination. The document should include the expression «freight prepaid», as it has already been paid in origin.

It is appropriate to use the CFR rule when sales transactions occur during the sea journey, since it provides that delivery must be made on board the ship or "by providing the goods so delivered", i.e. once shipped and given that the bill of lading acts as a negotiable instrument.

Customs clearance

The application of the CFR rule requires the selling party to carry out export clearance, where applicable, in the country of origin's customs.

For its part, the buying company shall be responsible for the import customs procedures in the country of destination and, where appropriate, transit procedures through third countries.

The selling company must provide the buyer with the documentation it requests for carrying out such procedures and the payment of their costs.

Modes of transport and goods

The CFR rule is used in the sale of very different types of goods, from those which are transported as bulk, breakbulk or general cargo (boxes, drums, bales, sacks, etc., in single units or grouped on pallets), heavy machinery, bulky parts or containers, among others, provided that maritime transport is to be used for their shipment.

(Continued on page 84)

CFR (cost and freight)

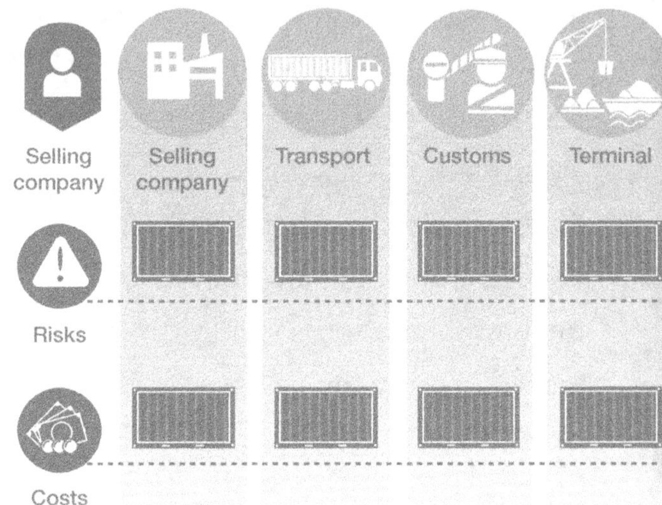

The seller bears the logistics costs until the goods are placed at the designated port of destination although the delivery and transfer of risks to the buyer occur once the goods are on board the ship at the port of embarkation.

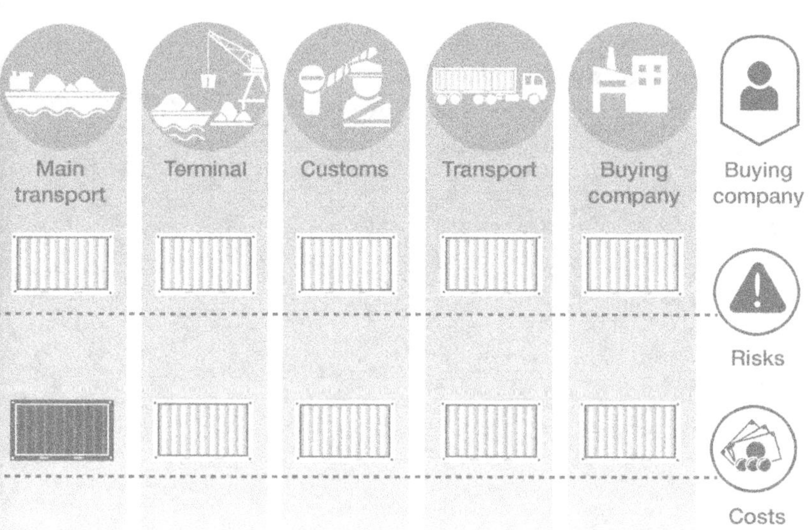

At the end of the maritime transport, the costs of unloading in the port of destination fall on the buying company unless the seller's contract of carriage includes them.

CFR (cost and freight): with container

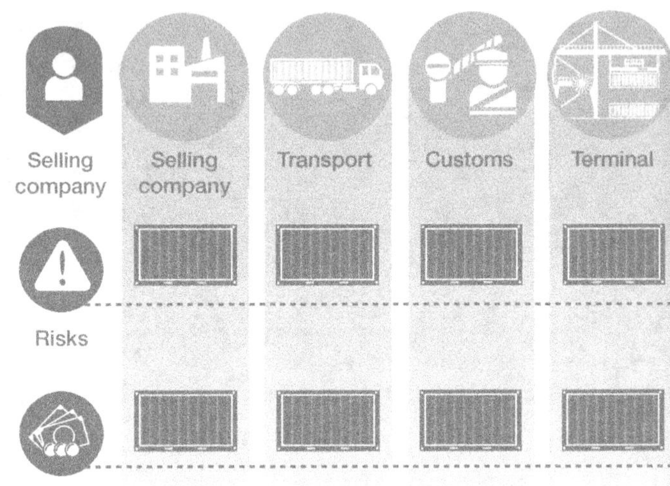

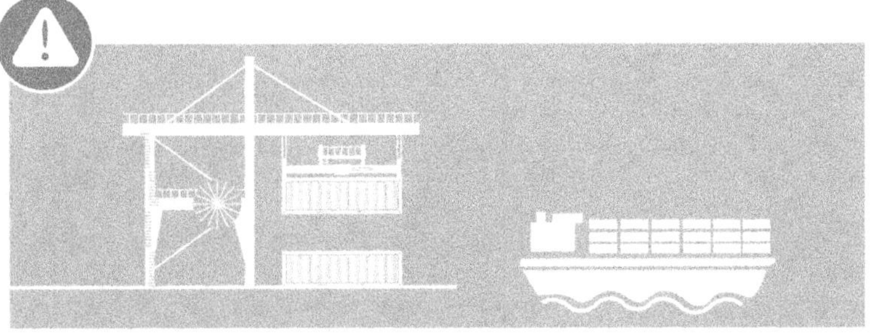

The seller bears the logistics costs until the goods are placed at the designated port of destination although the delivery and transfer of risks to the buyer occur once the container is on board the ship at the port of embarkation.

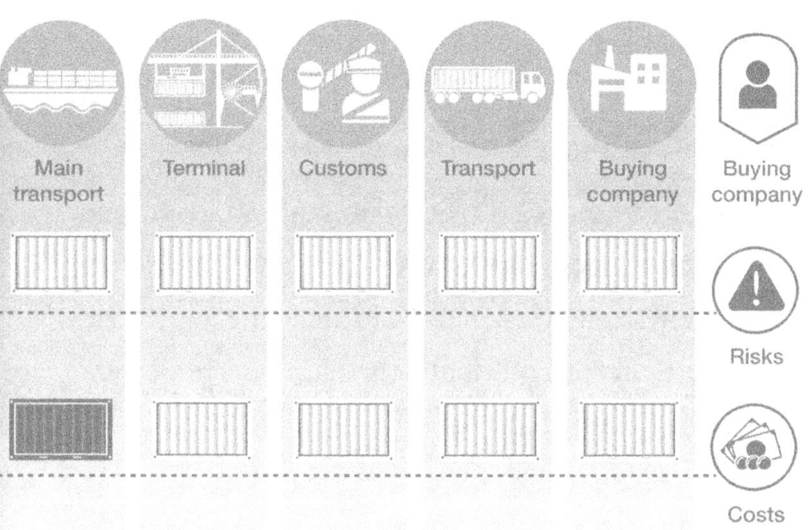

At the end of the maritime transport, the costs of unloading the container in the port of destination fall on the buying company, unless the seller's contract of carriage includes them, a fact that usually occurs when container transport services are booked under liner terms.

(Continued from page 79)

However, if the goods travel in a container, it is more advisable to use the CPT rule.

Insurance

The CFR rule does not oblige taking out an insurance policy but both companies have to decide whether to insure the risks of the operation, the seller until the goods are delivered on board the ship and the buyer from that moment on.

CIF (cost, insurance and freight)

Place of delivery and transfer of risks

Under the CIF rule, the selling company is obliged to bear all costs and freight necessary to transport the goods to the named port of destination, without unloading the goods from the ship. However, delivery and transfer of risk takes place once the goods have been placed on board the vessel. In the event of one or more transhipments of the goods in different ports during transportation, the goods are considered to be delivered in the first of them, the port of embarkation.

Since the selling company bears a significant part of the transport costs, with regard to the contractual clauses of loading and unloading or maritime transport shipping terms, it can book the freight under LIFO conditions (*liner in, free out*), which will include the cost of loading and stowage operations of the goods in the port of origin, while the unstowing and unloading at the port of destination will be borne by the buying company or its consignee.

Using the CIF rule, it is also possible to agree that the unloading costs at the port of destination are borne by the selling company, for which it is necessary to indicate the CIF *landed* condition and agree on the operation with the shipping company.

The selling company must provide the buyer with the standard transport document (originals of the maritime *bill of lading* or BL) which allows the latter to pick up the goods at the named port of destination. The document should include the expression «freight prepaid», as it has already been paid in origin.

It is appropriate to use the CIF rule when sales transactions occur during the sea journey, since it provides that delivery must be made on board the ship or "by providing the goods so delivered", i.e. once shipped and given that the bill of lading acts as a negotiable instrument.

Customs clearance

The application of the CFR rule requires the selling party to carry out export clearance, where applicable, in the country of origin's customs.

For its part, the buying company shall be responsible for the import customs procedures in the country of destination and, where appropriate, transit procedures through third countries.

The selling company must provide the buyer with the documentation it requests for carrying out such procedures and the payment of their costs.

Modes of transport and goods

The CIF rule is used in the sale of very different types of goods, from those which are transported as bulk, break-bulk or general cargo (boxes, drums, bales, sacks, etc., in single units or grouped on pallets), heavy machinery, bulky parts or containers, among others, provided that maritime transport is to be used for their shipment.

(Continued on page 92)

CIF (cost, insurance and freight)

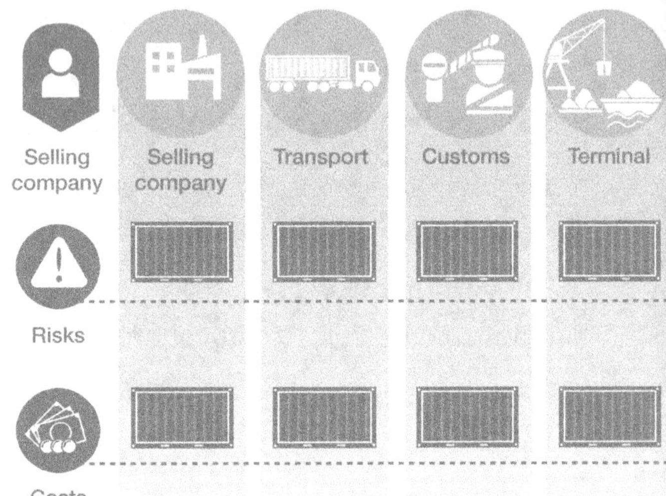

The seller bears the logistics costs until the goods are placed at the designated port of destination although the delivery and transfer of risks to the buyer occur once the goods are on board the ship at the port of embarkation.

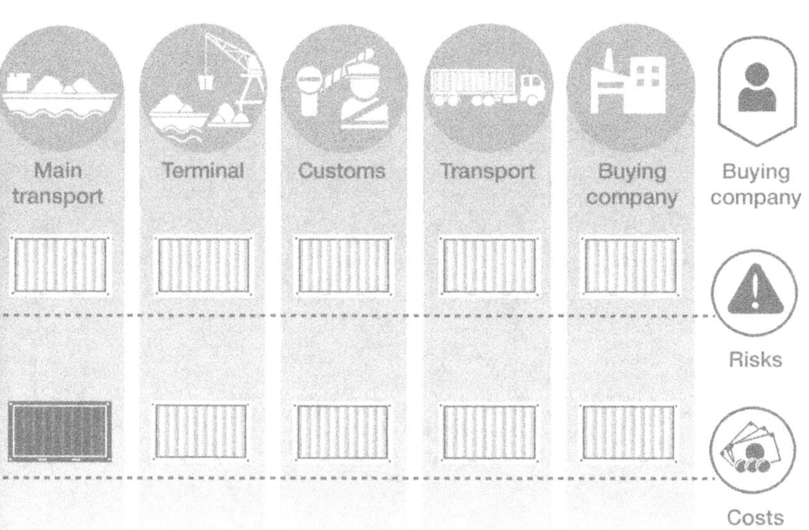

At the end of the maritime transport, the costs of unloading in the port of destination fall on the buying company unless the seller's contract of carriage includes them.

CIF (cost, insurance and freight): with container

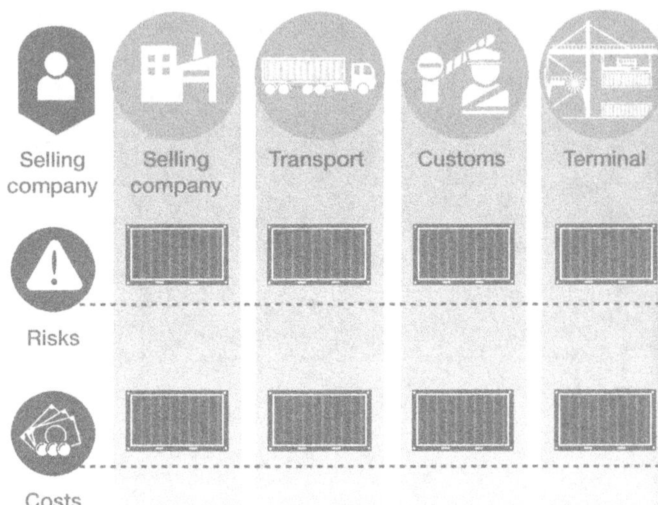

The seller bears the logistics costs until the goods are placed
at the designated port of destination although the delivery
and transfer of risks to the buyer occur once the container
is on board the ship at the port of embarkation.

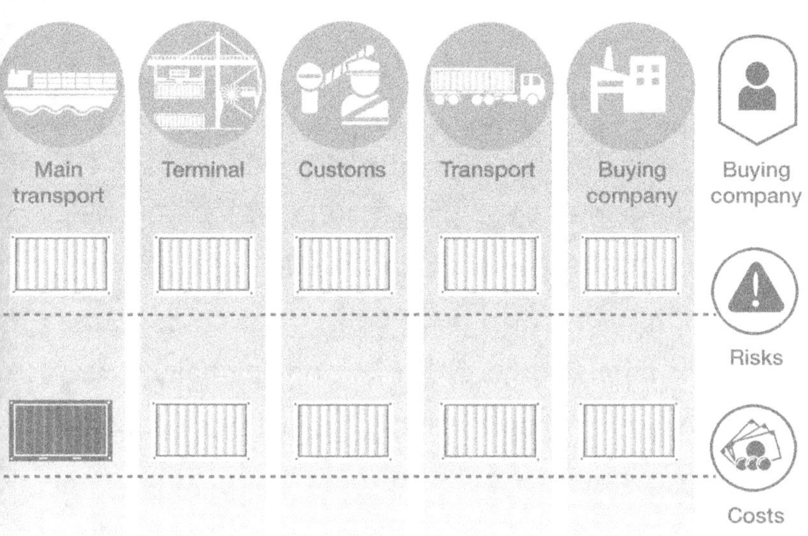

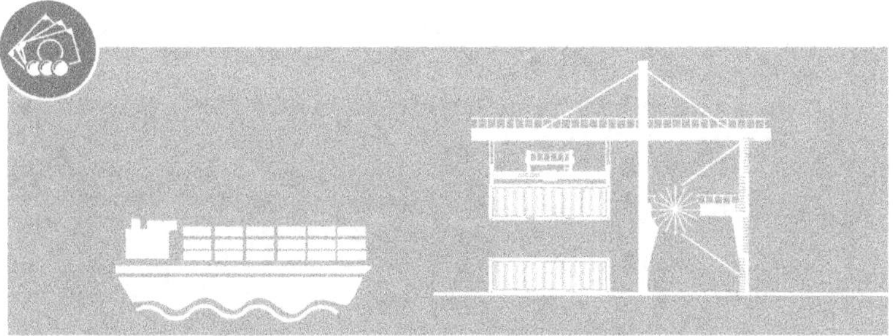

At the end of the maritime transport, the costs of unloading
the container in the port of destination fall on the buying company
unless the seller's contract of carriage includes them, a fact that
usually occurs when container transport services are booked under
liner terms.

(Continued from page 87)

However, if the goods travel in a container, it is more advisable to use the CPT rule.

Insurance

The CIF rule adds to the CFR conditions the obligation on the selling company to take out and assume the premium of an insurance policy that covers the risks of the goods borne by the buying company with respect to the transport, that is, from the shipment in the port of origin. Such insurance must provide the minimum coverage set out in the ICC (Institute Cargo Clauses) clauses of the London Institute of Insurers or similar. The insured amount must cover at least 110% of the price set in the sales contract and must be formalised in the same currency as the contract.

CPT (carriage paid to)

Place of delivery and transfer of risks

By using the CPT rule, the selling company is obliged to book and bear all the costs of the transportation of the goods up to the named place of destination (sea, land or air terminal) with the buyer, although the delivery and transfer of risks to the latter take place in origin, once the goods have been delivered to the carrier that the seller itself has hired. In the event that several carriers are involved in the transport, the goods are considered to be delivered to the first of them, in the seller's own premises or in the place that has been expressly designated.

The selling company must provide the buyer with the standard transport document (bill of lading in maritime transport, waybill in other modes of transport) for the hired transport.

Customs clearance

The application of the FOB rule requires the selling party to carry out export clearance, where applicable, in the country of origin's customs.

For its part, the buying company shall be responsible for the import customs procedures in the country of destination and, where appropriate, transit procedures through third countries.

The selling company must provide the buyer with the documentation it requests for carrying out such procedures and the payment of their costs.

Modes of transport and goods

The CPT rule is multimodal and may be applied to any mode of transport that is used or possible combinations among them (road, sea, air and rail).

It is advisable to use the CPT rule if the goods travel in container, either as full load (FCL) or as break-bulk (LCL), in which case it is not advisable to use the CFR and CIF rules.

Insurance

The CPT rule does not oblige taking out an insurance policy but both companies must decide whether to insure the risks of the operation, the seller until the delivery of the goods and the buyer from that moment on, when it assumes the set of remaining operations in the logistics chain to the destination.

CPT (carriage paid to)

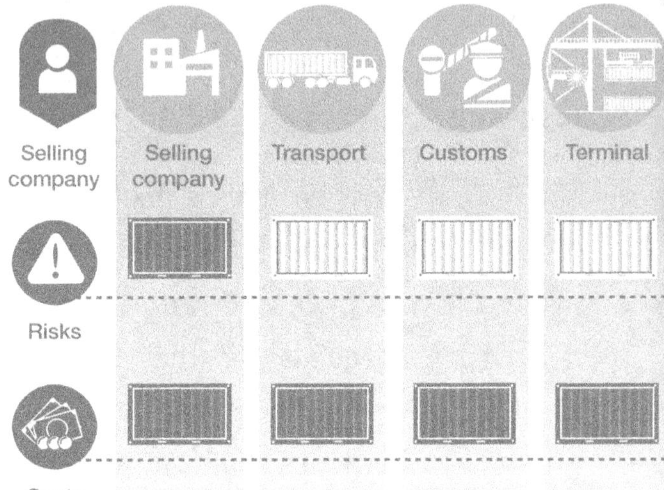

The selling company bears the transport costs to the designated place of destination (port or railway terminal, logistics center, etc.) although the delivery and transmission of risks to the buyer take place when the goods are made available to the first carrier at its facilities or another agreed place.

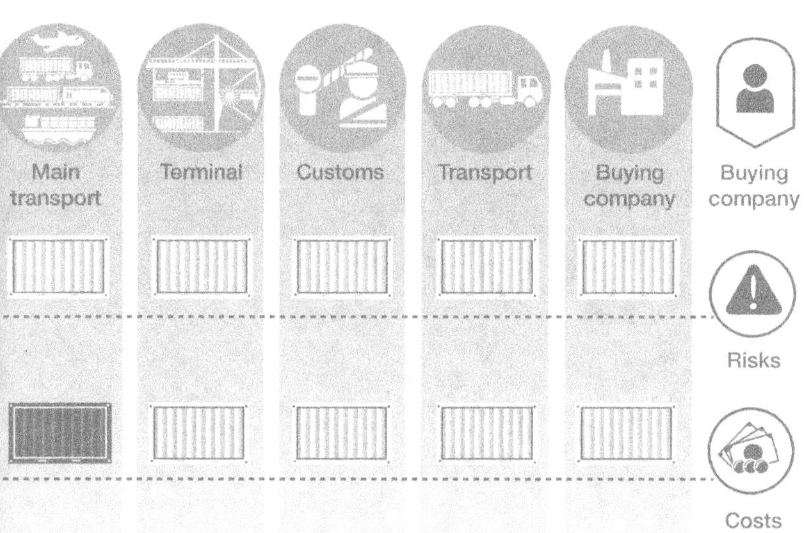

At the end of the maritime transport, the costs of unloading in the port of destination fall on the buying company unless the seller's contract of carriage includes them.

CPT by road (carriage paid to)

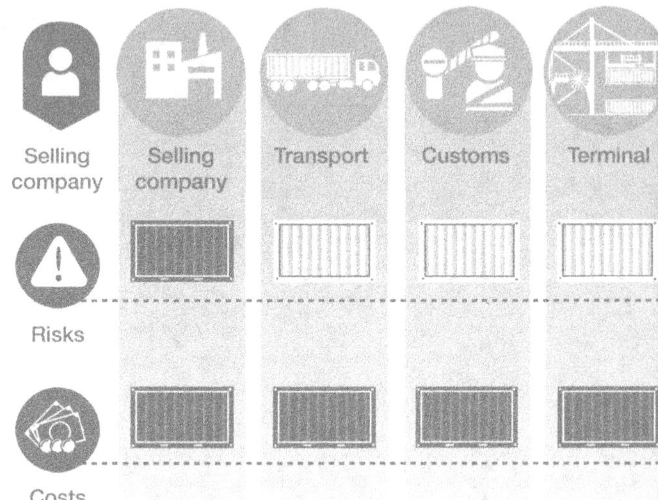

The selling company bears the costs of road transport
to the designated place (usually the buying company's premises)
although the delivery and transmission of risks to the buyer take
place when loading the goods on the carrier's vehicle at its premises
or another agreed place.

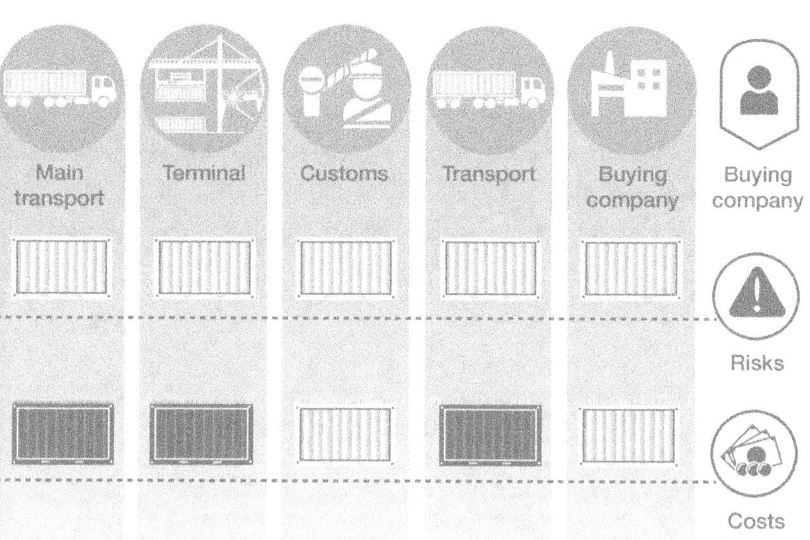

At the end of the road transport, the costs of unloading in destination fall on the buying company unless the seller's contract of carriage includes them.

CIP (carriage and insurance paid to)

Place of delivery and transfer of risks

By using the CIP rule, the selling company is obliged to book and bear all the costs of the transportation of the goods to the named place of destination (sea, land or air terminal) with the buyer, although the delivery and transfer of risks to the latter take place in origin, once the goods have been delivered to the carrier that the seller itself has hired. In the event that several carriers are involved in the transport, the goods are considered to be delivered to the first of them, in the seller's own premises or in the place that has been expressly designated.

The selling company must provide the buyer with the standard transport document (bill of lading in maritime transport, waybill in other modes of transport) for the hired transport.

Customs clearance

The application of the CIP rule requires the selling party to carry out export clearance, where applicable, in the country of origin's customs.

For its part, the buying company shall be responsible for the import customs procedures in the country of destination and, where appropriate, transit procedures through third countries.

The selling company must provide the buyer with the documentation it requests for carrying out such procedures and the payment of their costs.

Modes of transport and goods

The CIP rule is multimodal and may be applied to any mode of transport that is used or possible combinations among them (road, sea, air and rail).

(Continued on page 106)

CIP (carriage and insurance paid to)

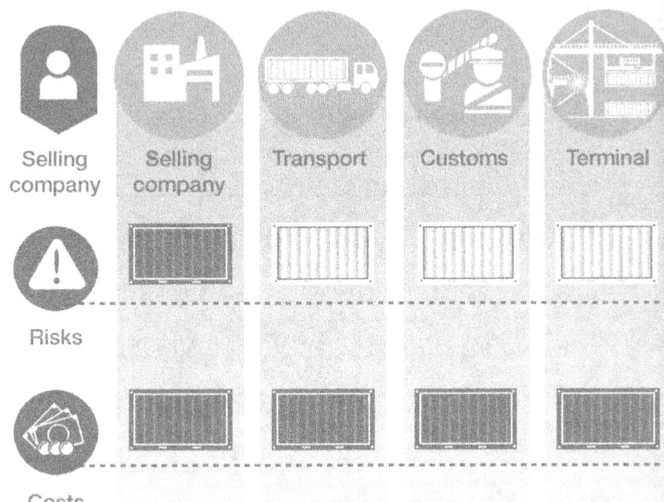

The selling company bears the transport costs to the designated place of destination (port or railway terminal, logistics center, etc.) although the delivery and transmission of risks to the buyer take place when the goods are made available to the first carrier at its facilities or another agreed place.

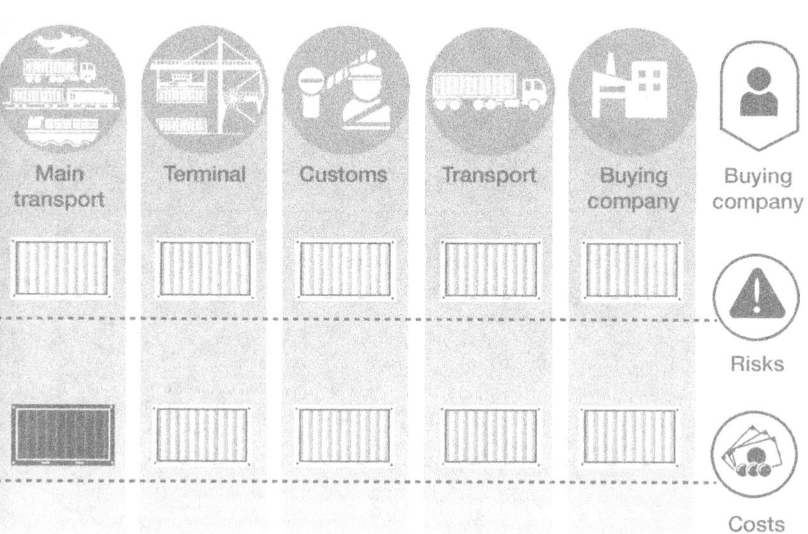

At the end of the maritime transport, the costs of unloading in the port of destination fall on the buying company unless the seller's contract of carriage includes them.

CIP by road (carriage and insurance paid to)

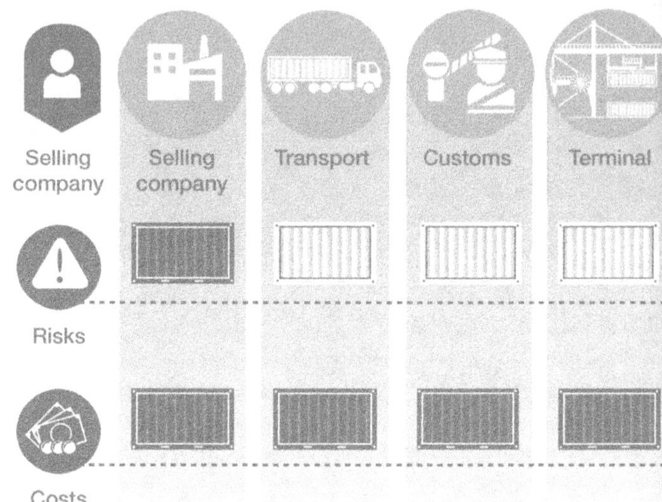

The selling company bears the costs of road transport
to the designated place (usually the buying company's premises)
although the delivery and transmission of risks to the buyer take
place when loading the goods on the carrier's vehicle at its premises
or another agreed place.

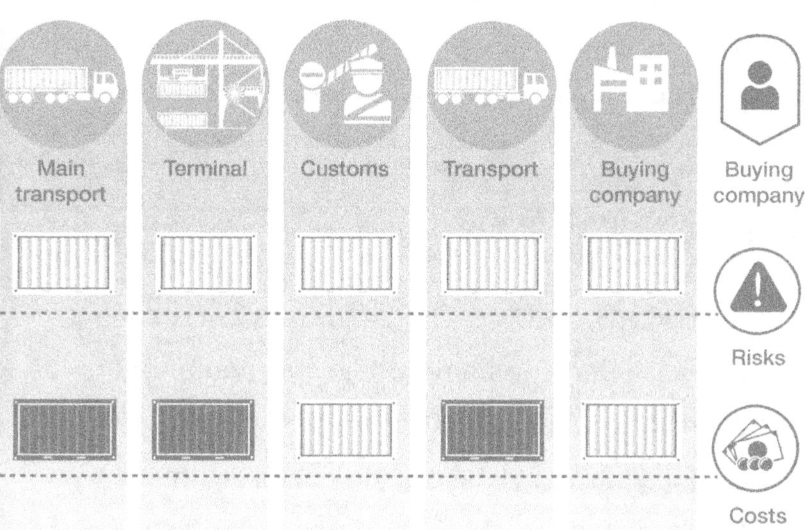

At the end of the road transport, the costs of unloading
in destination fall on the buying company unless the seller's
contract of carriage includes them.

(Continued from page 101)

It is advisable to use the CIP rule if the goods travel in container, either as full load (FCL) or as break-bulk (LCL), in which case it is not advisable to use the CFR and CIF rules.

Insurance

The CIP rule adds to the CPT conditions the obligation on the selling company to take out and bear the cost of an insurance premium that covers the risks of the goods borne by the buying company from the moment they are delivered to the carrier up to the place of destination where the seller has hired the transport (port or rail terminal, logistics center, etc).

Such insurance must provide the minimum coverage set out in the ICC (Institute Cargo Clauses) clauses of the London Institute of Insurers or similar. The insured amount must cover at least 110% of the price set in the sales contract and must be formalised in the same currency as the contract.

Delivery at destination

These delivery conditions are the ones that imply most responsibilities for the selling company, which bears all the costs and risks arising from the transport of the goods from the point of origin to the agreed place in the country of destination.

This group comprises the DAP, DPU and DDP multimodal rules.

DAP (delivered at place)

Place of delivery and transfer of risks

Under DAP terms, the selling company fulfills its delivery obligation and transmits the risks by placing the goods, on the means of transport and without unloading, at the disposal of the buyer at a designated point in the country of destination: port, factory, warehouse, depot, logistics center, etc. This way, the selling company must bear the risks and costs arising from all stages of transport up to the named place of delivery.

For its part, the buying company must provide the seller with proof of receipt of the goods. The selling company may even condition the payment of the last stage of transport (usually by road) to obtaining such proof to ensure that the goods have actually been delivered to the buying company in perfect condition and on the terms agreed with the carrier.

Customs clearance

The application of the DAP rule requires the selling party to carry out export clearance, where applicable, in the country of origin's customs.

For its part, the buying company will be responsible for the import customs procedures in the country of destination.

The selling company must provide the buyer with the documentation it requests for carrying out such procedures and the payment of their costs.

Modes of transport and goods

The DAP rule is multimodal and may be applied to any mode of transport that is used or possible combinations among them (road, sea, air and rail). However, it is particularly suitable when using full truck load or groupage road transport that does not require import customs clearance.

Insurance

The DAP rule does not oblige taking out an insurance policy but both companies have to decide whether to insure the risks of the operation, the seller until the goods are delivered, without unloading from the means of transport, and the buyer from that moment on.

DAP (delivered at place)

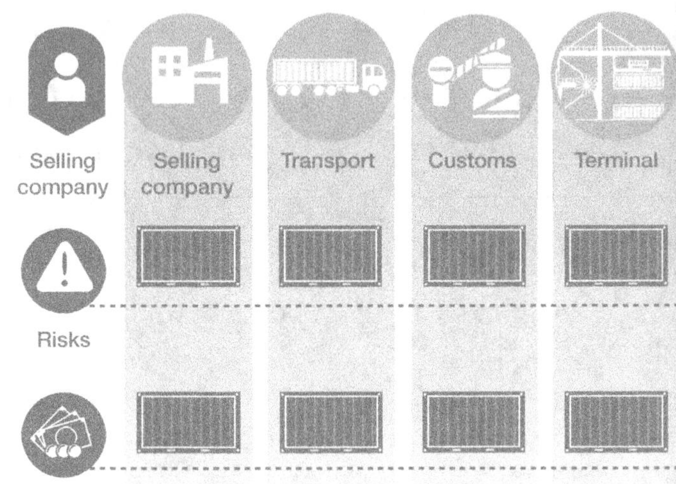

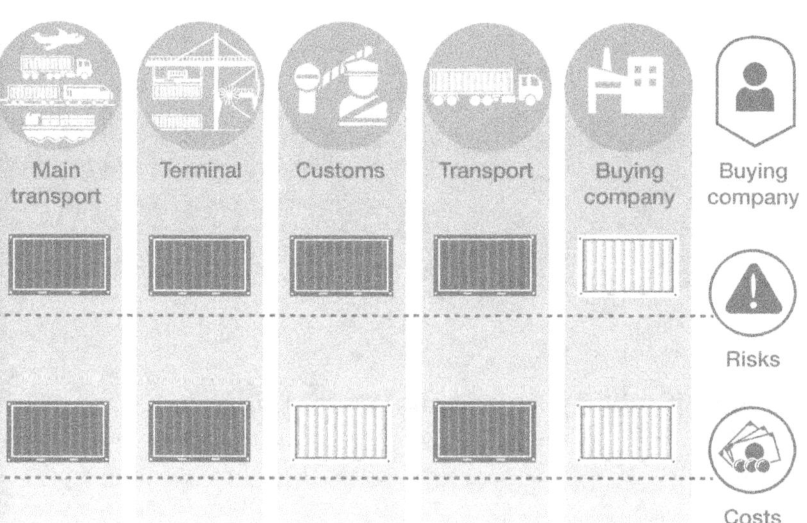

The selling company bears the costs and risks until the goods are delivered to the designated place of destination (terminal, logistics center, warehouse, etc.), without unloading them from the arrival vehicle. From that moment on, the costs and risks are borne by the buying company.

DPU (delivered at place unloaded)

Place of delivery and transfer of risks

Under DPU terms, the seller bears all the transport costs and fulfils its delivery obligation by placing the goods, unloaded from the means of arrival transport, at the disposal of the buyer at the place of destination named in the contract of sale (logistics center, buying company warehouse, etc), at which time they transfer the risks to the buyer.

For its part, the buying company must provide the seller with proof of receipt of the goods. Under the DPU rule, since the delivery takes place at destination, the selling company may even condition the payment of the main transport on obtaining such proof to ensure that the goods have actually been delivered in perfect condition and on the terms it has agreed with the carrier company.

Customs clearance

The application of the DPU rule requires the selling party to carry out export clearance, where applicable, at the country of origin's customs and, where appropriate, transit procedures through third countries.

For its part, the buying company will be responsible for the import customs procedures in the country of destination.

The selling company must provide the buyer with the documentation it requests for carrying out such procedures and the payment of their costs.

Modes of transport and goods

The DPU rule is multimodal and may be applied to any mode of transport that is used or possible combinations among them (road, sea, air and rail).

(Continued on page 118)

DPU (delivered at place unloaded)

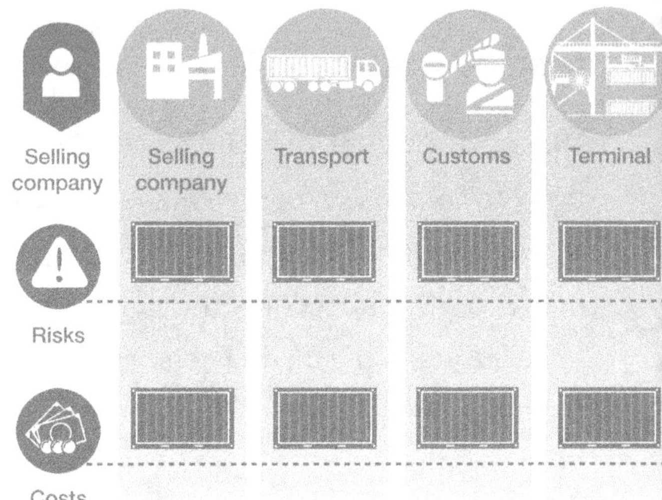

The selling company bears the costs and risks until the goods
are delivered to the designated place of destination (port or airport
terminal, logistics center, etc.), unloaded from the arrival vehicle.
From that moment on, the costs and risks are borne by the buying
company.

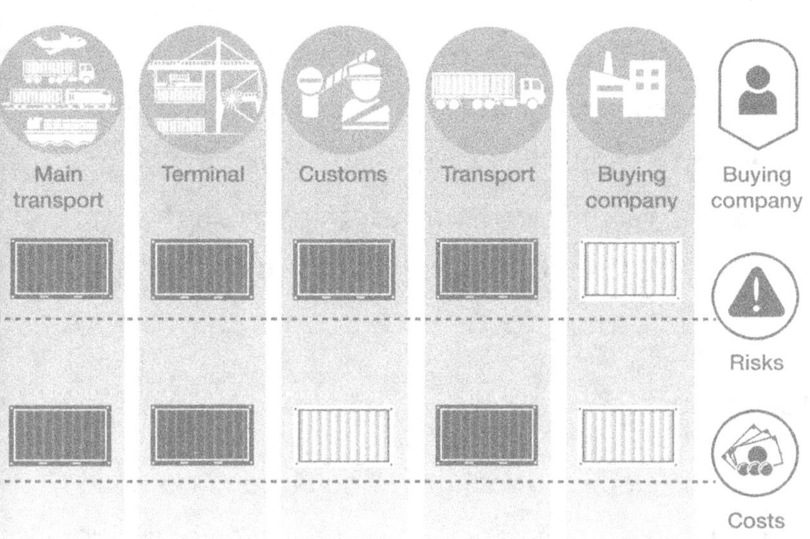

The selling company bears the costs and risks until the goods
are delivered to the designated place of destination (warehouse,
logistics center, etc.), unloaded from the arrival vehicle. From that
moment on, the costs and risks are borne by the buying company.

DPU (DELIVERED AT PLACE UNLOADED)

(Continued from page 115)

Among its applications, the DPU rule is suitable for parcel operations, in which the carrier takes charge of unloading the goods from the transport vehicle, or when it comes to breakbulk transported in a container that is broken down in the freight forwarding company's warehouse. On the contrary, it is not when it comes to transporting the goods by full truck load.

Insurance

The DPU rule does not oblige taking out an insurance policy but both companies have to decide whether to insure the risks of the operation, the seller until the goods are delivered and the buyer from that moment on.

DDP (delivered duty paid)

Place of delivery and transfer of risks

Under DDP terms, the selling company fulfills its delivery obligation and transmits the risks by placing the goods, on the means of transport and without unloading, at the disposal of the buyer at a point beyond the arrival terminal in the country of destination: factory, warehouse, depot, distribution platform, etc. This way, the selling company bears the risks and costs arising from all stages of transport up to the place of delivery agreed with the buyer.

(Continued on page 122)

DDP (delivered duty paid)

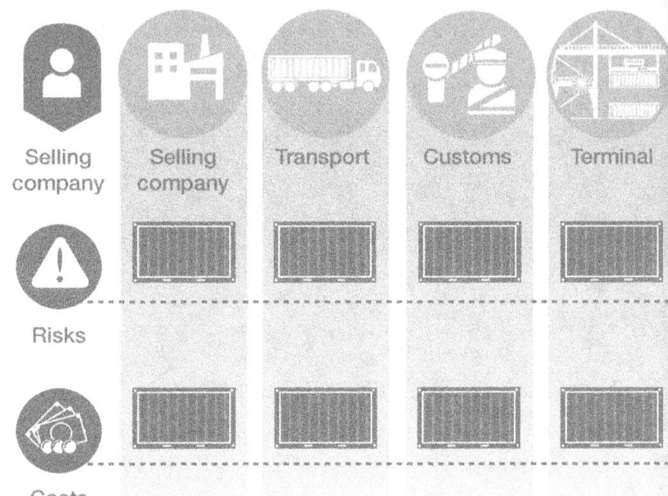

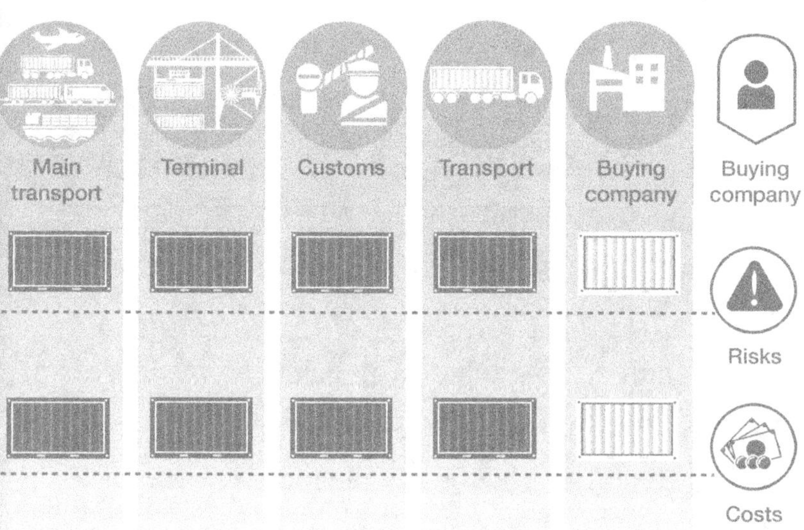

The selling company bears the costs and risks until the goods are delivered, import customs cleared, at the designated place of destination (the buying company warehouse or other), without unloading them from the arrival vehicle. From that moment on, the costs and risks are borne by the buying company.

(Continued from page 119)

For its part, the buying company must provide the seller with proof of receipt of the goods. The selling company may even condition the payment of the last stage of transport (usually by road) to obtaining such proof to ensure that the goods have actually been delivered to the buying company in perfect condition and on the terms agreed with the carrier.

If it is agreed to exclude the payment of any of the costs arising from the importation (e.g. VAT) from the obligations of the selling company, the DDP *VAT unpaid* or DDP *VAT excluded* reference must be clearly stated, as appropriate. In this way, the buying company assumes the payment of this tax.

Customs clearance

In addition to the management of export clearance by the selling company, the DDP rule adds to the DAP rule conditions the obligation on the latter to manage and assume import clearance and the taxes derived from it in the country of destination. These delivery conditions therefore imply the maximum obligations for the selling company.

Modes of transport and goods

The DDP rule is multimodal and may be applied to any mode of transport that is used or possible combinations among them (road, sea, air and rail).

Insurance

The DDP rule does not oblige taking out an insurance policy but both companies must decide whether to insure the risks of the operation, the seller until the delivery of the goods, without unloading from the means of transport, and the buyer from that moment on.

Collection: Gestiona
Director: David Soler

Practical guide to the Incoterms 2020 rules. Rights and obligations on the goods
in international trade
1st edition, 2021
© 2021, David Soler García
© 2021, including cover design, ICG Marge, SL
Original title in Spanish: *Guía práctica de las reglas Incoterms 2020*

Publisher: Marge Books
València, 558 – 08026 Barcelona
Tel. 931 429 486 - marge@margebooks.com
www.margebooks.com

Translator: Henry O'Donnell
Editorial collaboration: Alfonso Cabrera Cánovas, in the revision of the work,
  elaboration of the diagrams and writing of the accompanying notes.
Infographics: José Soto
Layout: Mercedes Lara
Printed by: Safekat, SL (Madrid)

ISBN printed edition: 978-84-18532-84-9
ISBN digital edition: 978-84-18532-85-6
Legal Deposit: B 13743-2021

The paper used in this book has not been bleached with elemental chlorine (Cl_2).

**Lean Services.
Certification Manual**

Luis Socconini

**Lean Manufacturing.
Step by step**

Luis Socconini

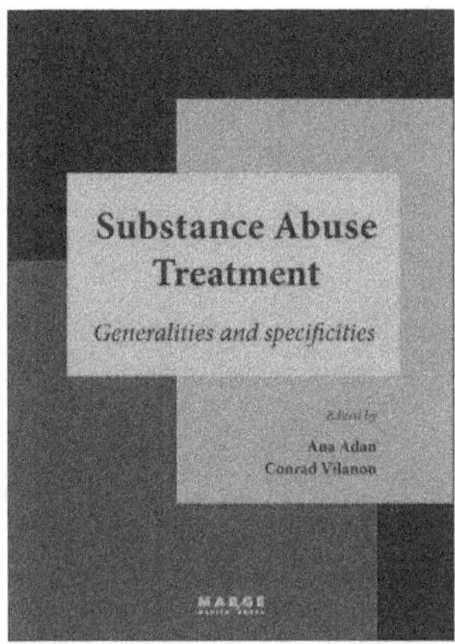

**Substance Abuse
Treatment**

Ana Adan, Conrad Vilanou

**Shipping & Commercial
Case Law**

Albert Badia

Lean Six Sigma.
Management System
for Leaders
Luis Socconini, Carlo Reato

Sales and operations
planning.
S&OP in 14 steps
Cristina Peña Andrés

Lean Six Sigma Yellow Belt.
Certification Manual
Luis Socconini

Practical guide to the
Incoterms 2020 rules
David Soler

València, 558 – 08026 Barcelona – Tel. +34-931 429 486 – marge@margebooks.com – www.margebooks.com

9 788418 532849